DOVER GAME AND PUZZLE ACTIVITY BOOKS

Mazes

DAVE PHILLIPS

DOVER PUBLICATIONS, INC.
New York

DOVER GAME AND PUZZLE ACTIVITY BOOKS

GENERAL EDITOR: BRIAN DOHERTY

Bibliographical Note

Mazes is a new work, first published by Dover Publications, Inc., in 1993.

International Standard Book Number: 0-486-27859-X

Manufactured in the United States of America
Dover Publications, Inc., 31 East 2nd Street, Mineola, N.Y. 11501

INTRODUCTION

WITH THIS COLLECTION, maze master Dave Phillips makes his debut in a compact new Dover format. You'll find the same wit and humor that Mr. Phillips has become known for—in a smaller, easier-to-carry format. These mazes are not the simple "get from point A to point B" variety. They require you to successfully perform certain tasks (explained in each caption). For example, you will be asked to find the one domino (among many) that, when knocked over, causes all the other dominoes to fall. In a more typical puzzle, you are to pass through a bowling ball and then five pins—and then through another ball and the remaining pins.

You will need to use your brainpower to solve these puzzlers—but hopefully you will not find that to be an entirely unpleasant sensation! Good luck and happy mazing!

FOOTPRINTS

Find a path that enters the maze, passes through all footprints and exits the maze without using any part of a path more than once. You must alternate between right and left prints.

VENDING MACHINES

Find a path that enters the maze, passes through all coins and vending machines and exits the maze without using any part of a path more than once. You must collect two coins before entering a vending machine.

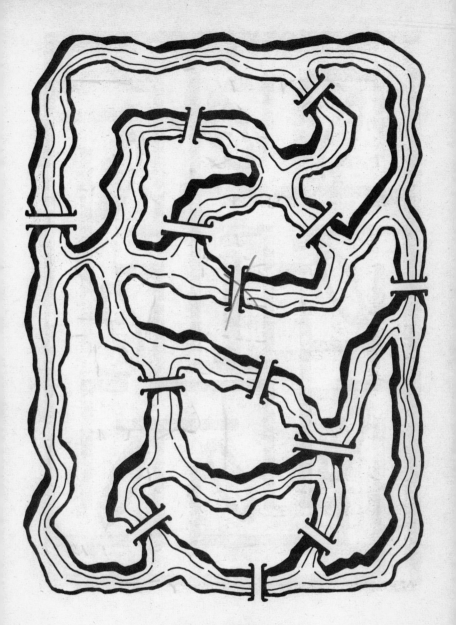

BRIDGE BUILDING

Where must you build a bridge so that you can visit each island only once?

RINGTOSS

Find a path that enters the maze, passes through all rings and the peg, and exits the maze without using any part of the path more than once. You must collect all rings before passing through the peg.

WATERWORKS

Find four separate paths that start at the water tower, pass through one faucet and then exit the maze without using any part of a path more than once.

GHOSTS

Find a path that enters the maze, passes through all ghosts and exits the maze without using any part of a path more than once. You may only pass through a ghost from behind.

SALAMANDER

Find a path that enters the maze, passes through the salamander, rocks and grass, and exits the maze without using any part of a path more than once. You must first pass through the salamander, then alternate between the grass and the rocks.

GEARS
Which gear must be removed so that all the rest will turn together?

DAISIES

Find a path that starts at any daisy, passes through all the other daisies and ends on the first daisy, without using any part of a path more than once. You must alternate between the two kinds of daisies.

TENPINS

Find a path that enters the maze, passes through a bowling ball, then through half the pins and exits the maze. Then find another path that passes through the remaining ball, then the remaining pins and also exits the maze. You may not use any part of a path more than once.

RIGHT TURN ONLY

Find a path that enters the maze, passes by all buildings and exits the maze without using any part of a path more than once. You may cross your path, but you can only go straight or turn right and you may not pass over an arrow in the wrong direction.

PIGS AND MUD

Find a path that enters the maze, passes through all pigs and the mud and exits the maze without using any part of a path more than once. Each pig must go to a mud puddle.

12

SEASONS

Find a path that enters the maze, passes through all trees and exits the maze without using any part of a path more than once. Start with any tree but you must then pass through the others in the correct seasonal order.

BLOCK HOPPING

Start with the man in the center. You must visit every block only
once and then jump off the mountain. You can only jump to an
adjacent block and no more than one block up or down at a time.

14

MAGPIES

Find four separate paths that enter the maze, pass through one magpie, then one coin and exit the maze. You may not use any part of a path more than once.

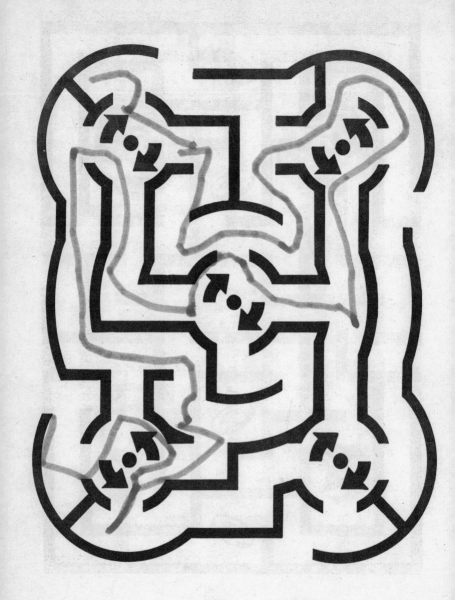

ROUNDABOUT

Find a path that enters the maze, passes through all arrows and exits the maze without using any part of a path more than once. You may only pass over an arrow in the direction it is pointing.

TWINS

Find two separate paths that enter the maze, pass through both the twins in each set and exit the maze without using any part of a path more than once.

PUNCH

Find a path that enters the maze, passes through the pitchers and glasses and exits the maze without using any part of a path more than once. First collect a pitcher, then pass through the right glasses to empty that pitcher. Each pitcher can fill two empty glasses. Note: four glasses are half-full.

MÖBIUS MAZE

Find the path that the four ants take if they all travel the same route without meeting, and without retracing their path, until they reach their original position. Keep track of which side of the path you are on.

KNIFE, FORK AND SPOON

Find a path that enters the maze, passes through all knives, forks and spoons and exits the maze without using any part of a path more than once. You must use the order: knife, fork, spoon.

FISH HEADS

Find a path that enters the maze, passes through all sea gulls and fish heads and exits the maze without using any part of a path more than once. Each sea gull must go to a fish head.

SNAKE PIT

Find which head belongs to which tail by following the paths as if they were the snakes' bodies. Do not make any turns a snake body cannot make and make sure snake bodies do not cross.

WINK

Find a path that enters the maze, passes through all eyes and exits the maze without using any part of a path more than once. You must alternate between open and closed eyes.

PLAID

Find three separate paths that join each pattern to its twin without using any part of a path more than once.

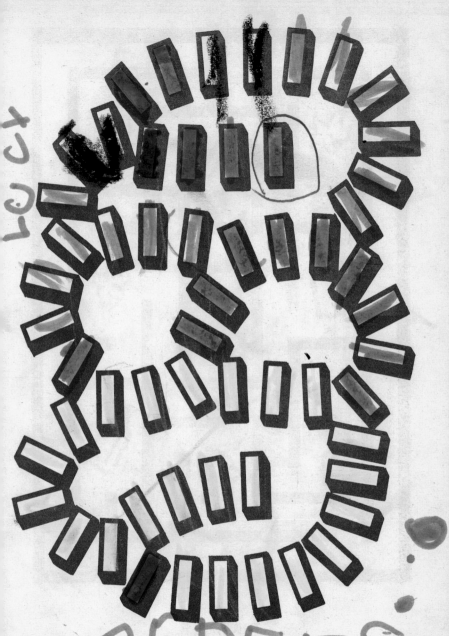

DOMINOES
Which domino must be knocked over so that all the rest will fall?

25

RECYCLE

Find a path that starts on any piece of garbage, passes through all the other garbage and ends on any other piece without using any part of a path more than once. You must collect all of one kind of garbage before collecting any other kind.

THIS WAY AND THAT

Find a path that enters the maze, passes through all double arrows and exits the maze without using any part of a path more than once. You must enter an arrow in the middle and exit in one of the directions an arrow is pointing.

MELONS

Find a path that enters the maze, passes through all melons and bags, and exits the maze without using any part of a path more than once. You must collect a bag and then two melons.

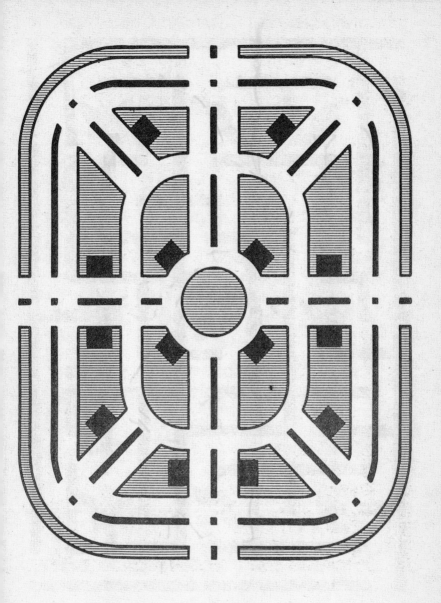

DELIVERY ROUTE

Find a path that enters the maze, passes by all buildings and exits the maze without using any part of a path more than once. Your path may cross itself but you must stay in the right lane and you may not take a left turn.

METAMORPHOSIS

Find a path that enters the maze, passes through all caterpillars, chrysalises and butterflies without using any part of a path more than once. You must use the order: chrysalis, caterpillar, butterfly.

LIZARDS

Find a path that enters the maze, passes through all lizards and exits the maze without using any part of a path more than once. You may not collect a lizard head on.

31

ROCK HOPPING

Children come down to this stream to hop from rock to rock. Find the path they take if they start and finish on the same bank and visit each rock only once.

AGING

Find a path that enters the maze, passes through all ages and exits the maze without using any part of a path more than once. You must pass through the ages in the correct order. Note that there are two consecutive "age sequences" in this maze, both of which are: baby (bald), young man (with hair), middle-aged man (mustache) and old man (beard).

TRAIN TRACKS

Two trains enter this maze and continue on their way without
crossing each other's path or using any section of the other's track.
You can only make turns a train can make and you cannot back up.

UP AND DOWN

Find a path that enters the maze, passes through all arrows and exits the maze without using any part of a path more than once. You must alternate between up and down arrows.

ASTEROID FIELD

These four spaceships must destroy all the asteroids. Each ship fires only two shots. Each shot travels in a straight line, destroying all asteroids in its path. You can only shoot along the white paths and you may not hit an asteroid more than once.

SNAKES ALIVE

Find a path that enters the maze, passes through all snakes and exits the maze without using any part of a path more than once. You may not collect a snake head on.

CHECKER DOTS

Find a path that starts on a square, visits all the other squares once, finishing on the last square, by moving horizontally or vertically one square at a time and only to the square "color" indicated by the dot.

DIAMONDS

Find a path that enters the maze, passes through all diamonds and exits the maze without using any part of a path more than once. Your path may cross itself, but you must travel in a straight line and change direction only on a large diamond. You may not pass through a diamond more than once.

PEACE

Find a path that enters the maze, passes through all peace symbols and exits the maze without using any part of a path more than once. You must alternate between the two symbol types.

SOLUTIONS

Footprints, *page 1*

Vending Machines, *page 2*

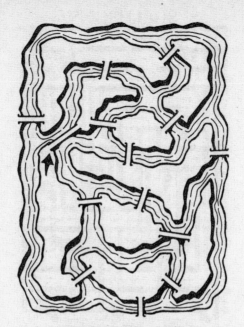

Bridge Building, *page 3*

Ringtoss, *page 4*

Waterworks, *page 5*

Ghosts, *page 6*

Salamander, *page 7*

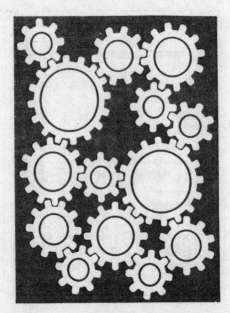

Gears, *page 8*

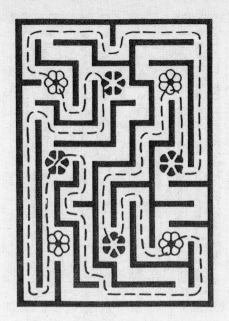

Daisies, *page 9*

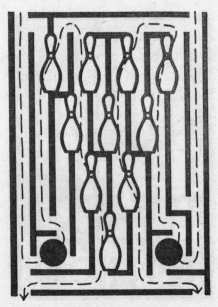

Tenpins, *page 10*

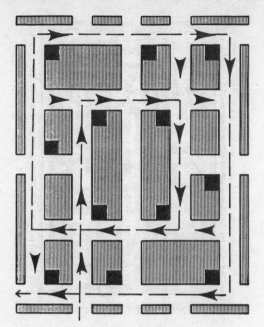

Right Turn Only, *page 11*

Pigs and Mud, *page 12*

Seasons, *page 13*

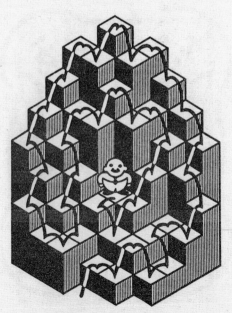

Block Hopping, *page 14*

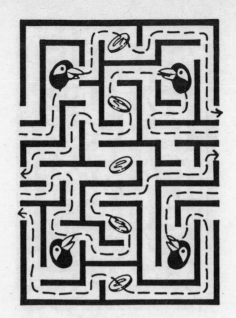

Magpies, *page 15*

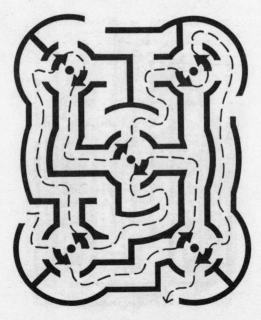

Roundabout, *page 16*

Twins, *page 17*

Punch, *page 18*

Möbius Maze, *page 19*

Knife, Fork and Spoon, *page 20*

Fish Heads, *page 21*

Snake Pit, *page 22*

Wink, *page 23*

Plaid, *page 24*

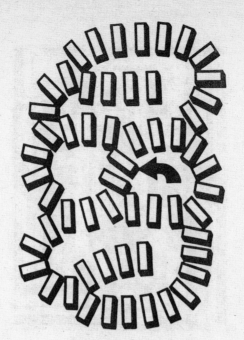

Dominoes, *page 25*

Recycle, *page 26*

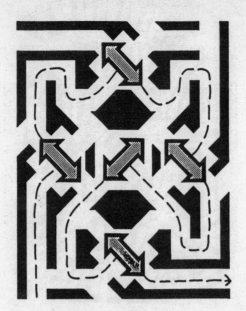

This Way and That, *page 27*

Melons, *page 28*

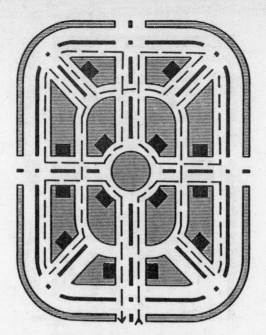

Delivery Route, *page 29*

Metamorphosis, *page 30*

Lizards, *page 31*

Rock Hopping, *page 32*

Aging, *page 33*

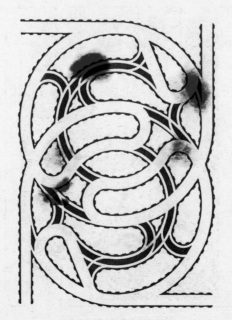

Train Tracks, *page 34*

Up and Down, *page 35*

Asteroid Field, *page 36*

Snakes Alive, *page 37*

Checker Dots, *page 38*

Diamonds, *page 39*

Peace, *page 40*